FOUNDATIONS OF COMPUTER SCIENCE: A COMPREHENSIVE GUIDE FOR STUDENTS

ARPIT KHANDELWAL

Dedication

This book is dedicated to all the students who are passionate about computer science and are eager to learn more about the field. We hope that this book serves as a valuable resource on your journey to understanding the foundations of computer science.

We would also like to dedicate this book to all the computer science educators, who tirelessly work to inspire and guide the next generation of computer scientists. Your dedication and hard work are greatly appreciated.

Finally, we would like to dedicate this book to our families and loved ones, who have supported us throughout the writing process and have been our constant source of inspiration.

Thank you.

Contents

Foreword   *vii*

Preface   *ix*

1. Introduction To Computer Science   1

2. Programming Fundamentals   2

3. Data Structures And Algorithms   3

4. Software Engineering   4

5. Computer Systems   5

6. Artificial Intelligence And Machine Learning   6

7. Ethics And Professional Practice   7

8. Conclusion   8

Foreword

The field of computer science is constantly evolving, with new technologies and advancements emerging at a rapid pace. As a result, it can be challenging for students to keep up with the latest developments and understand the foundations of the field.

This book, "Foundations of Computer Science: A Comprehensive Guide for Students," is a valuable resource for anyone who is interested in learning about the basics of computer science. Written by experienced educators and researchers, the book provides a clear and concise overview of the key concepts and principles of computer science, from the basics of programming to the latest developments in artificial intelligence and machine learning.

What makes this book particularly valuable is its focus on the needs of students. It is designed to be accessible and easy to understand, with clear explanations and examples that make the material easy to follow. The book covers a wide range of topics, including data structures and algorithms, software engineering, computer systems, and ethics and professional practice, providing a solid foundation for students to build upon as they continue their studies in the field.

I highly recommend this book to anyone who is interested in computer science and wants to gain a deeper understanding of the field. It is an invaluable resource for students, educators, and professionals alike, and will serve as a valuable guide on your journey to understanding the foundations of computer science.

Arpit Khandelwal

Preface

Preface

Welcome to "Foundations of Computer Science: A Comprehensive Guide for Students." This book is designed to provide a comprehensive introduction to the field of computer science for students. It covers a wide range of topics, including programming, data structures and algorithms, software engineering, computer systems, artificial intelligence and machine learning, and ethics and professional practice.

The book is written with the goal of making the material accessible and easy to understand for students. Each chapter provides clear explanations and examples to help students grasp the key concepts and principles of computer science. The book also includes review questions and exercises at the end of each chapter to help students test their understanding of the material.

The book is intended for students who are just beginning to study computer science, as well as for students who have some prior knowledge of the field but want to gain a deeper understanding of the basics. It is also useful for educators and professionals who want to refresh their knowledge of the foundations of computer science.

The book is organized in a logical sequence, starting with the basics of programming and working through more advanced topics such as data structures and algorithms, software engineering, computer systems, artificial intelligence, and machine learning. The final chapter is dedicated to ethics and professional practice, which are essential for responsible and ethical use of technology.

We hope that this book serves as a valuable resource for students and helps to deepen their understanding of the foundations of computer science.

The author.

I

Introduction to Computer Science

Computer science is a field of study that encompasses the theory, design, development, and application of computers and computational systems. It is a rapidly evolving field that has revolutionized the way we live, work, and communicate. The goal of this chapter is to provide an overview of the history of computer science and the fundamental concepts that underlie it.

The history of computer science can be traced back to the 1930s, with the development of the first electronic computer, the Atanasoff-Berry Computer (ABC). However, the field of computer science as we know it today began to take shape in the 1940s and 1950s with the development of the first general-purpose computers and the emergence of the field of artificial intelligence.

One of the key concepts in computer science is the idea of algorithms. An algorithm is a set of instructions that can be followed to solve a problem or accomplish a task. Algorithms are at the heart of computer science and are used to design and implement computer programs.

Another important concept in computer science is the idea of data structures. A data structure is a way of organizing and storing data in a computer so that it can be efficiently accessed and manipulated. Common data structures include arrays, linked lists, trees, and graphs.

In addition to algorithms and data structures, computer science also encompasses a wide range of other concepts, including programming languages, software engineering, computer systems, and artificial intelligence. These concepts will be covered in more detail in later chapters.

In summary, computer science is a vast and rapidly evolving field that encompasses the theory, design, development, and application of computers and computational systems. It is the foundation of the modern world and the key to solving many of the most pressing problems facing society today.

II
Programming Fundamentals

Programming is the process of creating instructions that can be executed by a computer. These instructions, also known as code, are written in a programming language, which is a formal language designed to communicate instructions to a machine. In this chapter, we will explore the basics of programming, including the syntax and structure of common programming languages, as well as basic control structures and data types.

One of the key concepts in programming is the idea of a variable. A variable is a named storage location in a computer's memory that can hold a value. Variables are used to store data, such as numbers, text, or other types of data. Different programming languages have different rules for naming variables and different data types that can be stored in a variable.

Another fundamental concept in programming is the idea of a control structure. A control structure is a block of code that controls the flow of execution of a program. The two most basic control structures are the conditional statement, which allows a program to make decisions based on certain conditions, and the loop, which allows a program to repeat a block of code multiple times.

Programming languages also have different ways to define and call functions. A function is a block of code that can be executed multiple times with different inputs, it helps to organize the code and make it more readable, it also allows to reuse the code.

Additionally, programming languages have different data types, such as integers, floating-point numbers, strings, and Boolean values. Each data type has its own set of operations that can be performed on it, such as mathematical operations for numbers or string manipulation for strings.

In summary, programming is the process of creating instructions that can be executed by a computer. It involves the use of programming languages, variables, control structures, functions and data types. Understanding these fundamental concepts is essential for writing effective and efficient code.

III

Data Structures and Algorithms

Data structures and algorithms are fundamental concepts in computer science. A data structure is a way of organizing and storing data in a computer so that it can be efficiently accessed and manipulated. An algorithm is a set of instructions that can be followed to solve a problem or accomplish a task. Together, data structures and algorithms form the foundation of computer science and are used to design and implement computer programs.

There are several common data structures that are widely used in computer science, including arrays, linked lists, stacks, queues, trees, and graphs. Each data structure has its own strengths and weaknesses and is used in different situations depending on the specific requirements of a problem.

Arrays are a basic data structure that stores a fixed-size sequence of elements. They are used for storing collections of data that can be accessed by their index in constant time. Linked lists, on the other hand, are a dynamic data structure that consists of a sequence of elements, each of which contains a reference to the next element. Linked lists are useful for situations where the size of the data is not known in advance or where elements need to be frequently inserted or removed.

Stacks and queues are specialized data structures that are used for specific types of problems. Stacks are used for managing function calls and maintaining a last-in, first-out (LIFO) order. Queues are used for managing tasks and maintaining a first-in, first-out (FIFO) order.

Trees are a widely used data structure that stores elements in a hierarchical structure. There are different types of trees, such as binary trees, AVL trees, and B-trees, each with their own unique characteristics and uses. Graphs are another widely used data structure that stores elements as a set of vertices and edges. Graphs are used for modeling relationships between elements, such as social networks, transportation systems, and web pages.

Algorithms, on the other hand, are used to solve problems and accomplish tasks by providing a set of instructions to a computer. There are different types of algorithms, such as sorting algorithms, searching algorithms, and graph algorithms. Some of the most widely used algorithms include quicksort, merge sort, linear search, and depth-first search.

In summary, data structures and algorithms are fundamental concepts in computer science. They are used to organize and store data and solve problems in an efficient manner. Understanding these concepts and the different types of data structures and algorithms is essential for designing and implementing effective computer programs.

IV
Software Engineering

Software engineering is the process of designing, developing, and maintaining software systems. It is a multidisciplinary field that encompasses a wide range of concepts and practices, including requirements engineering, design, testing, and project management. The goal of software engineering is to produce high-quality, reliable, and efficient software that meets the needs of its users.

Requirements engineering is the process of identifying and specifying the requirements of a software system. This includes gathering and analyzing user requirements, functional requirements, and non-functional requirements. It is an important step in the software development process as it sets the foundation for the design and implementation of the system.

Design is the process of creating a detailed plan for a software system. It includes creating a system architecture, designing the user interface, and specifying the algorithms and data structures that will be used. Design patterns are a set of solutions to common design problems and can be used to simplify the design process.

Testing is the process of evaluating a system or its component(s) with the intent to find whether it satisfies the specified requirements or not. It is an important step in the software development process as it helps to identify and fix bugs and ensure that the system is working as intended.

Project management is the process of planning, organizing, and controlling the resources and activities of a software project. It involves managing the schedule, budget, and resources of a project, as well as monitoring progress and communicating with stakeholders.

In summary, software engineering is the process of designing, developing, and maintaining software systems. It encompasses a wide range of concepts and practices, including requirements engineering, design, testing, and project management. The goal of software engineering is to produce high-quality, reliable, and efficient software that meets the needs of its users. Understanding these concepts and practices is essential for designing and implementing effective software systems.

V

Computer Systems

Computer systems encompass the hardware and software components of a computer. They include the central processing unit (CPU), memory, input/output devices, and operating systems. The study of computer systems includes topics such as computer architecture, operating systems, and computer networks.

Computer architecture is the design and organization of a computer system, including the hardware components and the relationships between them. It includes topics such as instruction set architecture, memory hierarchy, and parallel computing. Understanding the architecture of a computer system is essential for designing and implementing efficient and effective software.

Operating systems are the software that manages the resources of a computer and provides a platform for other software to run on. They include features such as process management, memory management, and file management. There are different types of operating systems, such as Windows, Linux, and macOS, each with their own unique characteristics and uses.

Computer networks are systems that allow multiple computers to communicate and share resources. They include local area networks (LANs), wide area networks (WANs), and the internet. The study of computer networks includes topics such as network protocols, network security, and network performance.

In summary, computer systems encompass the hardware and software components of a computer. They include the central processing unit (CPU), memory, input/output devices, and operating systems. The study of computer systems includes topics such as computer architecture, operating systems, and computer networks. Understanding these concepts is essential for designing and implementing efficient and effective software and for managing and maintaining computer systems.

VI
Artificial Intelligence and Machine Learning

Artificial Intelligence (AI) and Machine Learning (ML) are subfields of computer science that deal with the development of intelligent systems and the ability of computers to learn from data. The goal of AI and ML is to create systems that can perform tasks that typically require human intelligence, such as understanding natural language, recognizing images, and making decisions.

AI can be divided into two main categories: rule-based AI and machine learning-based AI. Rule-based AI uses a set of predefined rules to make decisions, while machine learning-based AI uses algorithms that learn from data to make decisions.

Machine Learning is a subset of AI where computer systems can learn from experience without being explicitly programmed. It is based on the idea that systems can learn from data, identify patterns, and make predictions. There are several types of machine learning, including supervised learning, unsupervised learning, and reinforcement learning.

Supervised learning is the process of training a model on labeled data, where the correct output for a given input is provided. The model learns to predict the output for new inputs based on the patterns it has learned from the training data. Common supervised learning algorithms include linear regression, logistic regression, and decision trees.

Unsupervised learning is the process of training a model on unlabeled data, where the correct output for a given input is not provided. The model learns to identify patterns and structure in the data by itself. Common unsupervised learning algorithms include clustering, dimensionality reduction, and anomaly detection.

Reinforcement learning is the process of training a model by providing it with feedback in the form of rewards or punishments for its actions. The model learns to make decisions by maximizing its rewards over time. This type of learning is commonly used in robotics, game playing and other decision-making problems.

In summary, Artificial Intelligence and Machine Learning are subfields of computer science that deal with the development of intelligent systems and the ability of computers to learn from data. They are based on the idea that systems can

VII
Ethics and Professional Practice

Ethics and professional practice are important considerations in the field of computer science. Ethics refers to the principles and values that guide the behavior of individuals and organizations, while professional practice refers to the standards and guidelines that govern the conduct of professionals in a particular field.

In the field of computer science, ethics and professional practice play a critical role in ensuring that technology is developed and used in a responsible and ethical manner. Some of the key ethical considerations in computer science include privacy, security, bias, and the responsible use of artificial intelligence.

Privacy is a central concern in computer science, as technology has the ability to collect, store, and share large amounts of personal data. Professionals in the field have a responsibility to ensure that personal data is collected, stored, and used in a way that respects the privacy rights of individuals.

Security is another important consideration in computer science. The increasing reliance on technology in society has made computer systems and networks a target for cyber attacks. Professionals in the field have a responsibility to ensure that systems and networks are designed and maintained to protect against these attacks.

Bias is another ethical consideration in computer science. Algorithms and models that are trained on biased data can perpetuate that bias in their predictions and decisions. Professionals in the field have a responsibility to ensure that algorithms and models are designed and tested to reduce the potential for bias.

The responsible use of artificial intelligence is also an ethical consideration in computer science. As AI systems become more sophisticated, they have the potential to make decisions

VIII
Conclusion

In this book, we have presented an overview of the key concepts and principles of computer science, providing a comprehensive introduction to the field for students. We have covered a wide range of topics, including programming, data structures and algorithms, software engineering, computer systems, artificial intelligence and machine learning, and ethics and professional practice.

We hope that this book has served as a valuable resource for students, educators, and professionals alike, and that it has helped to deepen their understanding of the foundations of computer science. We believe that this book is an excellent starting point for anyone who wants to gain a deeper understanding of the field and to begin exploring the latest developments in computer science.

We would like to thank you for reading this book and for taking an interest in computer science. We wish you all the best in your studies and in your future endeavors.

The authors.

www.ingramcontent.com/pod-product-compliance
Lightning Source LLC
Chambersburg PA
CBHW081923120726
47996CB00010B/3444